Short Walks in Auckland

Dog Friendly
Part One

By Helen Wenley and Grace Haden

First published in 2013.

Copyright 2014 Unleashed Ventures Limited

Photography by Helen Wenley

Wenley, Helen
Short Walks in Auckland – Dog Friendly Part One (2nd edition)
ISBN 978-0-9941126-6-8

Auckland (N.Z.) – Travel/walks

While the author and publishers have made every effort to ensure the information in this book was correct at the time of going to press, they accept no responsibility for any errors that may have occurred or any injury or inconvenience that may result from following the information contained herein, Facilities, location or amenities can change over time, so it is recommended that the reader call the operator or service and confirm any information that might be required.

For current rules and locations for off leash dog exercise areas, please refer to the Auckland Council website.

Map source: openstreetmap.org

Auckland Public Transport Buses and Trains information: www.maxx.co.nz

ABOUT AUCKLAND

New Zealand consists of two main islands with unimaginative names - the North Island and the South Island.

Auckland sits on an isthmus in the North Island between two harbours - Waitemata Harbour to the north and Manukau Harbour to the south.

The population of Auckland is higher than any other New Zealand City - just over 1.4 million currently. It's still a small city on a global basis.

There have been many tourists who have thought that New Zealand was connected to Australia by a bridge and yet others like a relative of mine who admired the view from the Sky Tower over lunch and confused the Waitemata Harbour with Cook Strait (the waters between the North and South Island).

Auckland is a city with lots of green spaces and native bush. There are many walks within Auckland away from the hustle and bustle of city life. There are some areas that are so close to residential houses or city streets and yet, you could feel very isolated because of the surrounding native bush.

Short Walks in Auckland aims to get you closer to Auckland, to learn about the history, the people, the geography, the geology, the flora and fauna, historic places and many other surprises which even well seasoned locals will be surprised to find.

We wish to encourage you to get out and about; to discover Auckland on foot, so that you can feel a real sense of belonging, appreciation and excitement about what this unique and diverse city has to offer.

Why short circular walks?

We appreciate that many of you have busy lives, and do not have the time to head out of Auckland to spend a whole day walking. These walks have been compiled to help you explore and learn about your local area in small bites. If as a family you choose to do these walks with young children, then we hope that the walk's brevity will inspire them to continue walking and walk further when they become adults, as well as provide happy family memories.

The circular concept allows you the freedom to start the walk at any point along the route. Once you are familiar with the route, you can change it around by extending it, shortening it and of course walking in the reverse direction. You could even become creative and link one circular walk to another nearby circular walk.

We have documented over 100 short circular walks in Auckland. You can download individual walk self-guide brochures from our website: *www.walksinauckland.com*

Walks with Dogs

Auckland Council has designated dog friendly off leash exercise areas throughout Auckland. To help you discover these areas for your dog, we have included them in our circular walks (check the current regulations at the Auckland Council website - see the Resources section at the end of this book).

The walks do include areas where your dog is required to be on leash, under control and used to road traffic. As a dog owner you will be familiar with the on and off leash signs used by the Council.

We have provided a list of dog friendly beaches in the "Resources" section.

This book is the first of three books of dog friendly books. Each walk provides a different aspect of Auckland's urban landscape, to help you and your furry companion discover new mini adventures. As with all our circular walks, start and end points can be varied.

Getting Started...

Keep your dog/s in sight and under effective control in off leash areas.

Dog droppings must be removed.

Dogs are not permitted on sport fields or near children's playgrounds.

Wear comfortable shoes to avoid sore feet (in winter prepare for mud and puddles).

Take water to sip, especially on hot summer days, for you and your dog.

Use sunscreen even on cloudy days.

Build up slowly if it's been a while since you exercised (take rest stops – most times you will find a park bench, and remember it's not a race!)

Walk with a 4 legged and/or human companion.

CONTENTS

1 Big King Reserve
THREE KINGS (CENTRAL)

This walk commences at the Duke Street entrance off Mt Eden Road. This popular walk for dog owners explores the remains of the volcano, provides views of the city skyline and other volcanoes such as Mt Albert, Mt Roskill, Mt Eden, Mangere Mountain and Rangitoto Island. The off leash area is well used by the after-work crowd. The route takes you down through the local residential area and children's playgrounds.

The Three Kings area is a volcanic centre formed 15,000 years ago when the 300 meter deep crater filled with lava and built three scoria mounds and overflowed into a 10 kilometer "river" through Western Springs to terminate as the Meola Reef in the Waitemata Harbour. The reserve has been planted with many pohutukawa trees that look magnificent when fully in flower.

In the period of Maori settlement it was a Pa site, evidence of this can still be seen on the western slopes.

The land was acquired by Governor Fitzroy in 1845 and in 1922 it was purchased by the current owners, Winstone Ltd. The area is now Auckland's largest scoria quarry which has resulted in a large pit, and leaves Big King, which was gifted to Mt Roskill Borough Council in 1927, as the only remaining cone. Big King remains as a council reserve and hosts a Watercare reservoir at the top. A further Watercare reservoir is concealed on the slopes.

The Three Kings panorama 1920 Big King is in the centre. Courtesy of Auckland City Libraries

Wesleyan Missionary Society set up a Native Institution for training native teachers; this moved from Grafton to an 80 hectare farm and provided Christian education for young Maori and needy European children. It transferred to Paerata in the early 1920's; its former location is marked with a plaque on McCullough Ave.

Arthur S. Richards Memorial Park was formed during the late 1930's and the following decade as part of a major housing development by the State. The land was part of the site of the Wesley College and was declared Crown land in 1949; it is notable for its mature trees.

Nearby Walks: Mt Eden, Cornwall Park

Description: A mix of level paths, steep paths and steps. Not wheel-friendly. Moderate fitness. Suitable in dry weather.
To see: Volcanoes, gravel pit, parks and playgrounds, 1960's state housing. Wonderful views of Manukau Harbour, South Head and the Waitakere Hills.
Time: approx. 60 minutes.
Parking: Main carpark off Duke Street (off Mt Eden Road)

Cafés: Orvietto, Mt Eden Road and The Eiffel (further south down Mt Eden Road towards Mt Albert Road)
Public toilets: by Duke Street carpark.
Children's playgrounds: Arthur Richards Memorial Park, Robertson Reserve (off Smallfield Ave)
Dogs: Off- and On-leash areas
Picnic areas only available. Pick your favourite spot.

Directions:

Start from the carpark (Duke Street, Three Kings).

1. Follow the path straight ahead from the carpark.

2. At junction of 3 paths, take the lower path on left <

3. Follow the path around to the right >.

4. Veer to the right > again.

5. Enjoy the view from the top of Big King beside the water tower.

6. Head back down again and take the long path, 2nd on right >, alongside the quarry, heading south.

7. At the bottom of the steps, keeping to the right > hand side of the playing field in the natural bowl, exiting up the grassy hill track on the right, near the corner.

8. In Fyvie Ave turn left <.

9. Turn left < into Smallfield Avenue.

10. Turn right into Robertson Reserve by the playground. Walk alongside the fence on the left < beside the kindergarten.

11. Turn right > at exit into McCullough Ave.

12. Turn left < into Scout Ave, then right > into Arthur Richards Memorial Park.

13. Turn hard right > and walk along the fence line "off-path", on the grass at the edge of the park behind the houses (the path straight ahead leads to the playground).

14. Exit into McCullough Ave and turn right >.

15. Turn left into Fyvie Ave, and then left < back into Big King Reserve.

16. Follow the path which leads to Little King by keeping to the left <. Keep following the path to Little King and where it splits, take the right-hand > fork.

17. Exit into Duke Street and turn right > to return to the car-park.

Harmon Avenue
Fulljames Avenue
Barclay Avenue
Duke Street
Connolly Avenue
Daily Terrace
Harmon Avenue
aron Avenue
Arthur
S Richards
Memorial
Park
McCullough Avenue
Parau Street
Big King
Reserve
Scout Avenue
McCullough Avenue
Robinson
Reserve
Fyvie Avenue
Smallfield Avenue

2 Newmarket Park

PARNELL (CENTRAL)

This walk starts off in the busy streets of Newmarket and heads to Parnell returning via the dog friendly off leash areas in Newmarket Park and Ayr Reserve.

Along the way you will see the historic Jubilee Building where Saturday morning markets are held. Then into Auckland Domain with a view of the Auckland Museum and a side trip to the Sensory Gardens. Then we cross the road to the Holy Trinity Cathedral and the promise of off leash romps.

Parnell is Auckland's oldest suburb; the settlement began in 1841. Maori occupied the area before the Europeans arrived. Parnell was named after Samuel Duncan Parnell, who is credited with the establishment of the Eight hour day in New Zealand.

Description: A mix of level paths, steps and slightly inclined paths. Suitable for users of average fitness and mobility. May require boots in wet weather, running shoes suitable in dry weather.

To see: Newmarket Broadway, Jubilee Building, Auckland Domain, Holy Trinity Cathedral, Ayr Reserve

Time: approx. 60 minutes. (about 4 kms)

Cafés: Various along route and Parnell

Public toilets: Newmarket Railway Station, Lumsden Green, Newmarket Park

Children's playgrounds: Newmarket Park

Dogs: Off leash in Ayr Reserve and Newmarket Park

Picnic Sites: Ayr Reserve, Newmarket Park

Nearby Attractions: Auckland Museum, Auckland Domain, Sensory Garden, Saturday morning   Farmers Markets (Jubilee Building), Parnell Village,   Holy Trinity   Cathedral

Directions:

Starting from Newmarket Railway Station.

1. Exit to the right > through the plaza and follow sign "to Broadway".
2. Exit right > onto Broadway and continue straight ahead.
3. Cross at the pedestrian lights opposite the Jubilee Building (Farmers Markets here on Saturday mornings).
4. Turn left > and then right > into the driveway in front of the Jubilee Building (Library and Community Centre).
5. Turn left < and continue through the carpark and turn right > into Titoki Street (to visit the Auckland Museum, Sensory Garden and Auckland Domain turn left < into Maunsell Road Extension).
6. Turn right > into Domain Drive, cross this road and continue to the right >.
7. Turn left < into Parnell Road (Optional: continue straight ahead to Parnell Village).
8. Cross Parnell Road at the St Stephens Road junction at the pedestrian lights, to the Holy Trinity Cathedral opposite .
9. Turn right > back down Parnell Road alongside the Cathedral.
10. Turn left < into Cathedral Place.
11. At the end continue straight ahead down the steps and along the track.
12. Turn right > at the T-junction.
13. At the culvert, keep to the right > and go up the steps.
14. At the top the hill, turn left <.
15. Turn right > up the wooden steps just before reaching the road.
16. Cross Ayr Street and enter Newmarket Park.
17. Turn left < alongside the children's playground (the pond is on your right>).

18. Turn left < and go up the incline.

19. At the top go straight ahead into Laxon Terrace (to the left < of the railway line). Continue straight ahead (Fumeaux Way, James Cook Crescent) and keep to the right-hand side footpath.

20. Turn right > up the path beside #24 James Cook Crescent (just before John Stokes Terrace on the left).

21. At the end of the path, cross over and follow the next path on the other side to the right>.

22. Return to Newmarket Railway Station.

3 Meola Reef

WESTERN SPRINGS (CENTRAL)

We begin the walk beside Western Springs Park and follow the path around the lake and then cross Motions Road to follow the path along the stream. Then down through Jaggers Bush Reserve and out through the off leash area, to come out on Meola Road. From there we enter Meola Reef Reserve (a popular off-leash fenced dog area). Gum boots are essential through the winter months. There is long grass, a muddy estuary, trees and a big field. We do the loop and return via Motat and back through Western Springs Park.

Meola Reef is a lava flow that came from the Mt St John, Mt Eden, One Tree Hill and Three Kings volcanoes and was formed 15,000 years ago when the 300 meter deep crater filled with lava and overflowed in a 10 Harbour. It is the longest lava flow in the Auckland volcanic field. The area around the reef is a 15-hectare reserve with stands of mangrove and salt marsh. Underground and above ground streams from Mt Albert, Mt Eden and One Tree Hill feed into the Harbour at Meola Reef.

Western Springs Park is a sanctuary for both people and wildlife. It surrounds a natural spring-fed lake, one of Auckland's early water supplies.

Nearby Attractions:

MOTAT (Museum of Transport and Technology)
Auckland Zoo

Description: Mainly level paths plus steps.

Suitable for most ages and levels of fitness and mobility, designed with flat shoes or running shoes in mind. Not suitable for wheelchairs and pushchairs.

To see: Waitemata Harbour views, a natural spring-fed lake with ducks, swans, geese and long-finned eels; stream, trams, planes.

Time: approx. 90 minutes.

Parking: Great North Road (Western Springs Gardens) opposite Western Springs.

Buses: Great North Rd. opposite Motions Rd

Cafés: None close by. Walk/drive/bus up Great North Road to Point Chevalier village, or drive/bus to Kingsland or Kings Plant Barn (St Lukes Road)

Public toilets: Western Springs beside the children's playground, Meola Reef.

Children's playgrounds: Western Springs – near entrance to Zoo carpark.

Dogs: Off-leash areas available at Meola Reef and Jaggers Bush.

Picnic Sites - Western Springs - BBQ's & tables near children's playground.

Nearby Walks: Grey Lynn Explorer, Westmere Loop Walk

Directions:

Start from the carpark in Great North Road.

1. Cross Great North Road to Western Springs Park.

2. Follow the path to the right > towards 'Stadium/MOTAT, lakeside walk'.

3. Turn right > at the lake edge.

4. Next junction turn left < and follow the lake edge all the way around until you reach the children's playground.

5. Straight ahead at the children's playground.

6. Exit at the Zoo's carpark and follow the exit road down to Motions Road.

7. Cross Motions Road to the other side (use the pedestrian island).

8. Turn left < then right > down the steps across the stream (Pasadena Walk).

9. Keep to the right-hand footpath and continue straight ahead, go past Pasadena Intermediate School.

10. Follow the path around the edge of school field (following stream).

11. At the end of the path cross the bridge and head back to Motions Road.

12. Turn left < and follow Motions Road past TAPAC.

13. Turn right > at MOTAT and head down the hill.

14. Go past Seddon Fields entrance.

15. Turn left < into Jaggers Bush (opposite Zoo Trade Entrance).

16. Follow the path straight ahead. After the bridge go up the steps to the right >.

17. Turn left < and follow the footpath alongside Meola Road.

18. Just past MOTAT entrance, cross Meola Road to a carpark and a Meola Reef sign.

19. Take the path on the left < of the car park (it's not obvious)

that goes into trees (not towards the Meola Reef Reserve sign).

20. Turn left < at the T-junction.

21. Straight ahead past the toilet block.

22. Go through the gate into dog off-leash area.

23. Straight ahead follow the fence line.

24. At the end of the path, keep going straight ahead to the gate in the far corner of the fence.

25. Head left < towards the end of the Point (and a rubbish bin).

26. Optional loop at the tip of the Meola Reef Point (with view of Auckland Harbour Bridge).

27. Turn right > and follow the path beside the rubbish bin, keep going straight.

28. Turn left < at second turning (back to entrance).

29. Cross Meola Road, turn left <, then right > into MOTAT – Meola Road entrance.

30. (You may wish to catch the tram back to Western Springs).

31. Follow the footpath past Western Springs College and TAPAC.

32. Cross Motions Road at pedestrian lights, and go straight ahead up the slope to re-enter Zoo carpark.

33. Head to far corner of the carpark back to the entrance of Western Springs lakeside.

34. Turn right > at the corner of the playground.

35. Keep to the left < for Great North Road.

36. Turn right > after crossing the double arched bridge.

37. Cross Great North Road to return to carpark.

.

4 Waiaturua Reserve

Waiaturua Reserve is an off road dog paradise. The dog friendly walking track circumnavigates the wetland reserve. You do have to keep your dog away from the wetlands area where there is protected birdlife. All dogs must be kept under control and within 10 metres of their owners.

It took 16 years to complete Waiatarua Reserve, the largest suburban constructed wetland in New Zealand, and it has won the Arthur Mead Environment Award awarded for excellence in sustainable environmental engineering.

Waiaturua's 57ha reserve used to be home to a 22ha wetland formed around 9000 years ago when a volcanic eruption isolated the catchment from the sea.

Description: Mostly level paths with very slight inclines. Suitable for users of average fitness and mobility. May require boots in wet weather, running shoes suitable in dry weather.

To see: Wetlands, Ducks and Pukeko bird's habitat.

Time: approx. 30-60 minutes depending on what you decide (about 3.3 kms)

Parking: Carpark off Grand Drive

Café: Hollywood Bakery, Lunn Avenue

Public toilets: In car park area

Children's playgrounds: Beside car park area

Dogs: Off leash on perimeter path

Picnic Site: Tables and seats scattered around reserve

Nearby Walks:

St Johns Explorer, Apirana St Johns Loop, Mt Wellington Explorer

Directions:

Start from Carpark off Grand Drive.

1. Take the path in right hand corner of car park opposite the playground.

2. Branch to the right > at the Y junction and go thru the stile at the gate.

3. Take the path to the right > over the bridge.

4. Continue straight ahead at next bridge, follow sign 'Wetland Walk Loop'.

5. Take right > turn to 'Gum Tree Walk' continue straight ahead.

6. Turn right > to rejoin main path.

7. Turn left < at the T-junction.

8. Turn left < to a lookout area and then retrace steps to main path, turn left <.

9. Turn left < opposite the bridge.

10. Turn right > onto the bridge that rejoins the main path.

11. Deviate onto the clay-ish path on the right > and head towards bridge that has a sign "No Swimming'.

12. Go past the picnic tables and rejoin the path to the left <.

13. Turn right > to return to the car park.

aiatarua Road
Keith Avenue
Loch Street
McFarland Street
Rosepark Crescent
Remuera Road
Honeyroyd Gardens
Monteith Crescent
Grand Drive
Towie Place
Wenvail Rise
Grand Drive
Waiatarua Reserve
P
Remuera Golf Course
Charles s
Winstone Drive
Start Here
Abbotts Way

5 Gittos Domain

BLOCKHOUSE BAY (CENTRAL)

This Blockhouse Bay circuit walk begins at the National Bank, winds through the newly renamed Gittos Domain (it was called Avondale South Domain) to Flounder Bay. It is an undulating short bush walk with steep paths and steps to test our fitness levels. There are many bench seats along the way. It is very peaceful with just the sound of birds. Many of the native trees have been sign-posted. At low-tide it is possible to walk along the edge of the Bays.

On Market Days (and each Tuesday) the Blockhouse Bay Historical Society opens the doors of Armanasco House (on the Village Green next to the library). We met Keith who explained to us that the old block house was a military building that was built so that it could withstand (or 'block') musket ball penetration. There were several block houses that were built in Auckland to protect the city from invasion during the Maori Wars.

The last Saturday of the month is Market Day in Blockhouse Bay's main street. At the street stalls you can buy fresh fruit and veggies, fish, delicious breads, plants, sweets, dog food and more.

Nearby Walks:

Blockhouse Bay Tiriwa Pathway, Lynfield Coast and Bush

Description: A mix of level paths and steep paths/steps. Suitable for users of average fitness and mobility. May require boots in wet weather, running shoes suitable in dry weather. Caution: Muddy and slippery when wet.

To see: Native bush, Manukau Harbour views

Time: approx. 45 minutes.

Parking: Blockhouse Bay Road

Cafés: various in Blockhouse Bay Road – we like 'The Block'

Public toilets: By the Village Green near the library

Children's playgrounds: None

Dogs: Off and On leash areas

Picnic Sites: Tables in Gittos Domain, many bench seats alongside track.

Directions:

Start from the National Bank (Blockhouse Bay Road).

1. Cross over Blockhouse Bay Road at the pedestrian crossing.

2. Turn right > and head south down Blockhouse Bay Road

3. Turn left < into Gittos Domain   and continue straight ahead

4. Turn right > at the crossroads (signs to Blockhouse Bay shops, Flounder Bay, Lewis St).

5. At top of the steps, continue straight ahead in front of the seat to steps down on other side

6. Turn right > at the next crossroads in between the seat and the rubbish bin

7. Turn left < at next junction signposted 'Blockhouse Bay Shops' (or if low-tide turn right > and you can walk along shore line to the bottom of Lewis Street)

8. Turn right > at next junction towards Blockhouse Bay Shops and Flounder Bay

9. Turn right > at the T-junction to Lewis Street and Flounder Bay

10. Enjoy the water view before turning left < up Lewis Street.

11. Re-enter Gittos Domain on the left < towards the top of Lewis Street

12. At the junction of steep downward steps, take the path to the left, at the bottom cross the bridge.

13. At the T-junction, turn right >

14. Return to the bank either via Countdown supermarket or the school.

25

Countdown
P
Start
here
Blockhouse Bay Road
Pioneer's
Mini Market
Blockhouse
Bay
School
Avondale
South
Domain
Gilfillan Street
Gill Crescent
Blockhouse Bay Road
Endeavour Street
Wade Street
Lewis Street

6 Belmont Bays

This is an on leash walk which we have included because of the wide open spaces. Part of this walk is along the Takapuna Cycle Route which currently extends from Esmonde Road to Victoria Road and the ferry in Devonport. The cycle route is paved and relatively flat, making it suitable for wheelchairs, pushchairs and a range of fitness levels. The cycle route stretches 6.8 km with a return walking trip taking around 3 hours.

Dogs are welcome along the walkway provided they are kept under control and do not disturb wildlife or other park users. Dogs are not permitted on sport fields or near children's playgrounds.

Description: A mix of level paths and slightly inclined paths. Suitable for users of average fitness and mobility.

To see: Estuary views, wetlands, residential housing, Auckland harbour Bridge

Time: approx. 45 minutes. (about 4.00 kms)

Parking: Corner Eversleigh Road & Rutherford Street

Cafés: Little&Friday in Eversleigh Road

Public toilets: None

Children's playgrounds: Northboro reserve, Bayswater park

Dogs: On leash only

Picnic Sites: Take a rug—picnic spots along route

Nearby Attractions:

Devonport, Mount Victoria, North Head, Narrow Neck Beach, Takapuna

Directions:

Start from Corner Eversleigh Road (off lake Road) & Rutherford Street.

1. Use the left-hand footpath along Rutherford Street and turn left < onto the pathway between the houses.

2. At the Northboro Reserve, keep to the right-hand path, then turn left < along the path below the playground.

3. Follow the cycleway/walkway, cross the long wooden bridge, past O'Neills Point Cemetery and Bayswater Park.

4. Cross over Bayswater Road and continue straight ahead.

5. Cross over Roberts Avenue and enter Plymouth Reserve. Continue along the grass track down the hill.

6. Join the main path and continue straight ahead to Casino Street

7. Turn right > into Roberts Avenue.

8. Turn left < onto the path that runs alongside the Bayswater Primary School playing field (nature walk).

9. Cross Bayswater Avenue and continue straight ahead into Moana Avenue.

10. Turn right > into Egremont Street.

11. Turn left < along Lake Road.

12. Turn left < into Bardia Street.

13. Turn right > into Coronation Street.

14. Return to the start.

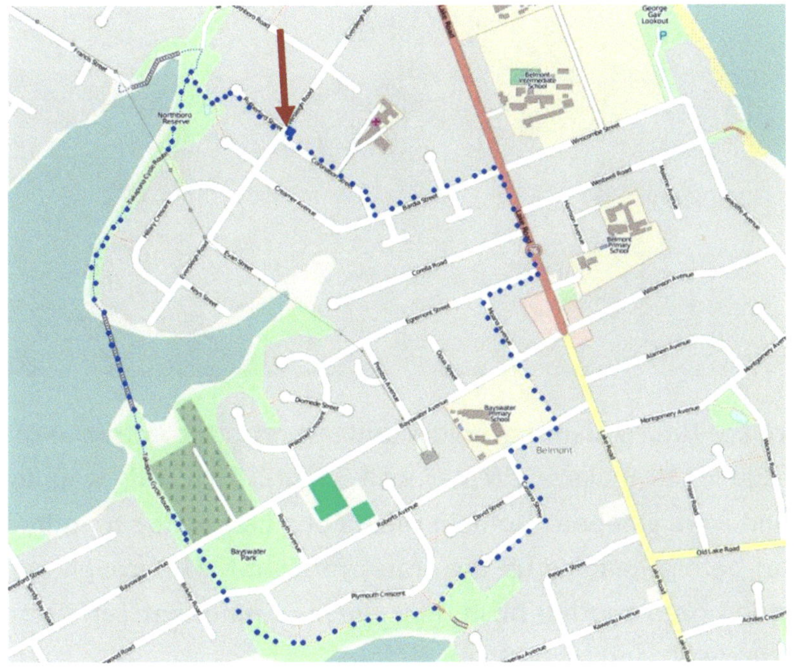

7 Northcote Tuff Crater

NORTHCOTE (NORTH)

There are future plans to build a bridge across the entrance to the Tuff Crater to make a circular walk. Until then, this walk loops around from Onepoto Domain then along half of dog friendly Tuff Crater before heading up the crater rim and back through streets and then onto another bush track. Bear in mind that Tuff Crater is a nature walk and home to many birds.

Onepoto Basin is another of Auckland's explosion craters and it is the oldest dated, erupting about 250,000 years ago. The Maori name "Onepoto" means small beach (named after Halls Beach near Northcote Point). There are plans to restore Tuff Crater, which is another explosion crater, to its natural state with a balanced ecosystem of native plants and wildlife, all with volunteer help. It was formed by explosive eruptions around the same time as Onepoto.

Description: Bush track, steps, inclines. Muddy in places when wet. Suitable for users of average fitness and mobility.

To see: Native bush, views across Auckland Harbour, native birds, volcanic crater

Time: approx. 60 minutes. (about 5.0 kms)

Parking: Onepoto Domain, Northcote.

Cafes: At Northcote Shopping Centre

Public toilets: Onepoto Domain

Children's playgrounds: Onepoto Domain, Heath Avenue reserve

Dogs: Off leash in Tuff Crater Reserve

Picnic Sites: Onepoto Domain

Nearby Walks: Northcote Point, Le Roys Bush, Takapuna

Directions:

Start from Onepoto Domain beside the Children's Playground.

1. Head into the playground area, and take the walkway to the left < between two play areas, keeping the big slide on your right >.

2. Follow the path which becomes a grassy track, cross over a narrow bridge and follow the path up the hill.

3. Turn left < into Sylvan Avenue.

4. Turn right > into Heath Avenue.

5. At the end of Heath Avenue follow the grassy walkway down to the reserve.

6. Cross the reserve to Exmouth Road and continue straight ahead along the track through Tuff Crater Reserve.

7. Exit the reserve and turn left < into Saint Peters Way (the road comes right down to the path where there is a wooden platform).

8. Turn left < up the walkway between #25 and #21.

9. Cross College Road and turn left <.

10. Turn left < along Exmouth Road.

11. Turn right > into Dudding Avenue.

12. Turn left < along walkway between #22 and #24.

13. Turn right > into Kororo Street.

14. Turn left < into Lake Road.

15. Turn left < Rotary Grove. Continue straight ahead along path alongside the swamp land to the very end.

16. Turn right > into Tarahanga Street.

17. Turn left < to enter Onepoto Domain and return to the start.

Greenslade Crescent
Lake Road
Potter Avenue
Coronation Road
Northcote Intermediate School
Cadness Street
College Road
Saint Peters Way
Kotanga Drive
Waiatarua Walk
Greenslade Reserve
P
P
P
Northcote Shops
Kilham Avenue
Northcote
Raleigh Road
Lake Road
Exmouth Road
Dewsbery Avenue
Araha Street
Foster gill
Dudding Avenue
Howard Road
Howard Road
Exmouth Road
McBreen Avenue
McBreen Avenue
Kororo Street
Rotary Grove
Lake Road
Onewa Road
Exmouth Road
Onepoto Domain
START
P
Toitoi Place
Puawai Place
Matanui Street
Northcote School
Taharoto Street
Heath Avenue
Sylvan Avenue
Onewa Road
421
Northern Busway
Auckland Northern Motorway
Onewa Road

8 Wattle Downs

WATTLE DOWNS (SOUTH)

The Wattle Downs Walkway goes around the edge of the peninsula that extends into Manukau Harbour, at one spot there are views through to Manukau Heads.

The walking route is also great for cyclists, and dogs on leash and an off dog leash area at Kauri Point Reserve. (Note: dogs are excluded in the Wattle Farm Reserve as it's a wildlife protection area).

There are many points of interest along the way, and friendly people to say hello to. We stopped and spoke to a resident whose house looked out towards Manukau Heads - he told us that they get to view amazing sunsets over the harbour.

There are wetlands and ponds active with shore birds - if you are a keen bird watcher, be sure to take your binoculars.

The walkway follows the coastal strip of reserve land adjoining the Wattle Downs residential area in Manurewa and the Papakura Stream. This walkway consists of esplanade reserve with two larger reserves at Kauri Point and adjoining Kaanapali Crescent. The Manukau Harbour is the dominant influence. Much of the land on the southern side of the Puhurehure inlet is rural, and boating activity on this part of the harbour is minimal. The coastal reserves provide a buffer between the residential uses and the habitat areas of the harbour edge. These mudflats are frequented by a range of wading birds such as oyster catchers and white faced heron.

Source: www.aucklandtransport.govt.nz/moving-around/walking-footpaths/MapsAndMore/Pages/WattleDownsWalkway.aspx

Nearby Walks:

Totara Park/Botanical Gardens
Conifer Grove Circuit

Description: Mainly level paths, one set of steps. Suitable for users of average fitness and mobility.

To see: Manukau Heads, Manukau harbour, wetlands, shore birds

Time: approx. 120 minutes. (about 8.5 kms)

Start: Wattle Farm Reserve, Wattle Farm Road

Cafés: None (shops in Coxhead Road)

Public toilets: Wattle Downs Park

Children's playgrounds: Various along route

Dogs: On and off leash areas

Picnic Sites: Seating along walkway

Directions:

Start: Wattle Farm Reserve carpark (off Wattle Farm Road)

1. Exit the Reserve via the carpark entrance.

2. Cross Wattle Farm Road and enter Wattle Farm Wetland Reserve. Follow the path straight ahead through the reserve.

3. Cross Tington Avenue and turn left <.

4. Turn right > onto the footpath through Tington Park – continue straight ahead past the playground.

5. Turn right > into Castlehill Court, then left < to exit Castlehill Court at Glenross Drive.

6. Cross Glenross Drive and follow path straight ahead to the waterfront.

7. Turn right > and follow the walkway around the waterfront (continue through Kauri Point Reserve) .

8. Turn left < into Sunningdale Street, then right > into Hadley Wood Drive.

9. Turn left < and follow the footpath alongside Scotsmoor Drive.

10. Continue straight ahead at the roundabout into Aberdeen Crescent.

11. Veer left < onto walkway off Aberdeen Crescent, continue straight ahead around the waterfront (ignore paths to the right).

12. At the t-junction of the paths, turn left < and keep taking the next left < turns.

13. Exit the walkway into Bluewater Place.

14. Turn left < into Wattle Farm Road.

15. Turn left < into Volante Avenue walkway (to avoid steps continue straight ahead along Wattle Farm Road).

16. Turn right > at the T-junction and follow the pathway down the steps to return to the start.

James Cook High School
Astor Place
Manukau Golf Course
Clayton Road
Wattle Farm Reserve
Start Here
Clayton Park School
McQuarrie Avenue
Acacia Cove Village
Wattle Downs
Aberdeen Cres
Sunberry Drive
Rotomoana Primary School
Guffy Place
Hadlee Field Drive
Sunnynglades Street
Blackwood Drive
Crabapple Road
Wattle Farm Road
Wattle Downs Golf Course
Kauri Point Reserve

9 Highbrook Park

HIGHBROOK (SOUTH)

The Highbrook area was developed as a racehorse stud farm before it was converted to a business park. This walk starts from within the streets, then leaves the buildings behind as we follow the Otara Creek and Tamaki River. The dog off leash area is by the Pukekiwiriki crater. The crater floor is now salt marsh and mangrove forest.

Pukekiwiriki ("the hill with the associated small lagoon") is a volcanic landform (a breached explosion crater and tuff ring), located at the end of the Waiouru Peninsula, on the north side of Otara Creek, at its exit to the Tamaki River (directly opposite the power station). As a result of submissions made by the Volcanic Cones Society, the proposed Highbrook Drive was moved slightly and most of the volcanic landform is within an attractive park at the end of the peninsula.

Description: A mix of level and slightly hilly paths. Suitable for users of average fitness and mobility. Suitable for mountain bikes.

To see: Pukekiwiriki Crater, wetlands, views of Tamaki Estuary, Otara Creek, Pakuranga Creek, Mount Wellington and other volcanoes, Highbrook Model Airpark.

Time: approx. 90 minutes. (about 6.0 kms)

Cafés: Sierra Café @ 52 Highbrook Drive
Public toilets: Sierra café
Children's playgrounds: None
Dogs: Off leash at Pukekiwiriki crater
Picnic Sites: Seating only in Highbrook Park

Nearby Walks:
Pakuranga Walkway, Mount Wellington Explorer

Directions:

Start at Landscaped Seating area, Corner Business Parade North and Highbrook Drive.

1. Turn up Business Parade South.

2. Cross over Underwood Street.

3. Turn left < into El Kobar Drive.

4. Cross over Pukekiwiriki Avenue to enter footpath straight ahead.

5. Follow pathway around the pond .

6. Turn left < after the pond and continue straight ahead.

7. Continue through wooden gate, and head to the pylons straight ahead.

8. At the pylons, turn right > onto the metal roadway.

9. Turn left < onto the footpath that takes you past the crater.

10. Cross over Highbrook Drive and enter the path on the right > into the reserve.

11. Follow the path as it parallels Highbrook Drive and the shore line.

12. As you approach Business Parade North, cut diagonally from the path up the slope towards a seating area surrounded by flax bush.

13. Cross over Highbrook Drive to return to the start.

Start
Here
Highbrook Drive
Highbrook Drive
Pukekiwiriki
Crater

10 Churchill Park

GLENDOWIE (EAST)

The big paddocks in Churchill Park have well-formed paths, little shade and is an off-leash area.

This walk begins on the corner of Roberta and Riddell Roads, traverses the nearby streets to enter the Park from Shrewsbury Avenue. From there we circumvent the paddocks, exiting into Riddell Road, then follow the coastal path back to the start.

The Auckland isthmus was rich in resources and a natural cross road for the many Maori tribes. Glendowie had particular importance as it commanded the inner Hauraki Gulf, and the entrance to the Tamaki river and routes south through to the South.

Crew from the Tainui Canoe settled in the area. In the mid eighteenth century the area became a battleground particularly at nearby Tahuna Torea sandspit and Karaka Bay.

In early European days the land was used as a farm by various early settlers, in 1923 area became a golf course but ran into financial strife and was purchased by a developer.

The 44 hectares of grazing farmland now known as "Churchill Park" was acquired by Auckland City Council in 1945, for a reserve and was named after Winston Churchill.

Nearby Attractions:

Karaka Bay. The site where the Treaty of Waitangi was signed here in a great ceremony by Governor Hobson and local Maori chiefs on 9th July 1840. **To get here you have to descend a zig-zag path.** Could be a good place for a picnic (and a swim) on a sunny day.

Description: A mix of level paths, and a few steep paths. Suitable in dry weather. Suitable for users of all ages and abilities, suitable for normal footwear and for wheelchairs and pushchairs.

To see: Sea views, city views, stream, private gardens, farm animals

Time: approx. 60 minutes.

Parking: On corner of Robert Ave and Riddell Road.

Café: Ronnie's Café, Corner of Riddell Road and Roberta Avenue

Public toilets: in reserve corner of Riddell Road & Roberta Ave

Children's playgrounds: Cnr of Riddell Road & Roberta Ave

Dogs: Off and On leash areas

Picnic Sites: take a rug and picnic basket, coffee flask

Nearby Walks: Tahuna Torea Nature Reserve, St Heliers and Glover Park

Directions:

Start from the corner of Roberta and Riddell:

1. Turn into Riddell Road, then left < into Hartland Ave.

2. Cross Whitehaven Road, then straight ahead into Shrewsbury Ave.

3. Enter the park beside the bowling club entrance, through the wooden gate on the right >.

4. At the next junction turn left<, and go through the gap in the thicket of trees.

5. Go through the swing gate, and turn left < after the second swing gate at the T-junction onto the main path.

6. The tennis club will be on your left. At the stock yard area, go through the gate and turn right > onto a concrete path.

7. Follow the path down the hill, round the corner and over the bridge past the nikau palms.

8. Follow the stream and go straight ahead at the junction that has a bridge on the left.

9. Turn right > opposite the Girl Guides Hall (beside the Scout Hall) and head towards Churchill Park School.

10. Turn right > at the next small path between two pine trees before the school.

11. Go through the stile that is to the right > of the school.

12. Keep following the main path.

13. Go straight ahead at the next cross-paths, then turn left < at the following one.

14. Take the next right > up the hill heading for the gate.

15. At the vista spot – enjoy the view of Waitemata Harbour and the city (stop for refreshments if you have a picnic).

16. Keep to the left hand path along the park perimeter. Exit the park at the next gate on the left < at the T-junction.

17. Turn left < into Riddell Road, then right > into Clouston Street.

18. At the end of Clouston Street, turn right > along the cliff top path.

19. Enjoy the harbour views before returning to the start.

20. Turn left < into Riddell Road.

11 Macleans Park

EASTERN BEACH (EAST)

Macleans Park is an off leash area at all times. It is the largest park in East Auckland and has well-maintained paths that wander over wide open pastures, ridges and small tracts of bush gullies. This walk loops around to Eastern beach. There are wonderful views out to sea.

Nearby Walks: Pigeon Mountain & Wetlands, Half Moon Bay

Description: A mix of level paths, steps and steep paths. Suitable for users of average fitness and mobility. May require boots in wet weather, running shoes suitable in dry weather.

To see: Hauraki Gulf/Tamaki Strait views, native bush, streams, beach

Time: approx. 60 minutes. (about 4 kms)

Parking: Macleans Road opposite Murvale Drive

Cafés: The Esplanade (to the left at Hostel Access Road).

Public toilets: The Esplanade

Children's playgrounds: The Esplanade

Dogs: Mostly off-leash (apart from along Eastern Beach)

Picnic Sites: Picnic tables on The Esplanade, Eastern Beach

Directions:

Start from Macleans Road opposite Murvale Drive.

1. Enter Macleans Park and take the path to the left <.

2. Turn right > at the fork near the school buildings, continue straight ahead along the path beside the fields.

3. Turn left < at the bottom of the hill.

4. Turn right > at the T-junction and continue straight ahead towards the Tamaki Strait.

5. Turn right > and go down the hill and then the steps.

6. Turn right > at the bottom of the steps and continue down Hostel Access Road.

7. Cross The Esplanade at the pedestrian crossing and turn right > along the waterfront.

8. Continue into the carpark at the end of The Esplanade, head towards the path that runs beside the public toilets following the sign to Awaroa Walkway.

9. Turn left < at the T-junction.

10. Take the path to the right > just before Bleakhouse Road.

11. Straight ahead at the next fork.

12. Turn right > up the rise.

13. Return to Macleans Road.

51

Vivian Wilson Drive
Rymer Court
Helen Place
Oakwood Close
Rogers Avenue
Eastern Beach
Oliver Road
The Esplanade
Bucklands Beach Road
Overley Court
Gifford Place
Eastern Beach
Villa Court
P
P
Wells Road
Macleans Road
Macleans Park
Oliver Twist Avenue
Bucklands Beach Intermediate
Macleans College
Richard Avenue
Charles Dickens Drive
Bucklands Beach Road
Copperfield Terrace
Pickering Drive
Galsworthy Place
Blackhouse Road
Crescent
Maugham Drive
MacLeans Road
MacLeans Rd
Start here

12 Moire Park

MASSEY (WEST)

Moiré Park is one of Waitakere's hidden gems. This walk passes through the bush of Moire Park alongside the Manutewhau stream and takes us through residential areas, parks and mangroves.

The park has many paths of different grades to suit all kinds of walkers. The walking circuit we have documented takes in the variety of the paths and scenery - from native bush to a hill view of the City. This is a dog friendly walk with a selection of off leash areas en route. There is a variety of playgrounds for children to enjoy and a BBQ and picnic area available. And a Pump Park for young cyclists.

More info and fun map from Waitakere City Council

www.waitakere.govt.nz/cnlser/pbr/prkgrnsp/pdf/moire-park-easy-walks-brochure.pdf

53

Nearby Walks:

Whau River-New Lynn Walk

Te Atatu Peninsula

Opanaku Stream

Description: A mix of level paths and steep paths. Suitable for users of average fitness and mobility. May require boots in wet weather, running shoes suitable in dry weather. Muddy tracks after rain.

To see: Auckland City views, Waitakere Hills view, native trees and fauna, urban development.

Time: approx. 75 minutes. (about 6 kms)

Parking: Westgate Shopping Centre

Buses: Westgate Shopping Centre

Cafes: Selection within Westgate Shopping Centre.

Public toilets: Moire Park.

Children's playgrounds: Moire Park, Katrina Esplanade, Elizabeth Ave, Flaunty Reserve, Midgely Road, West Harbour Esplanade.

Dogs: On and off leash.

Picnic Sites: Moire Park BBQ area. (Pump track for cyclists).

Directions:

Start from Main Street, Westgate Shopping Centre.

1. Walk down Main Street towards the yellow cycling/pedestrian bridge that leads off Westgate Drive.

2. Cross the yellow bridge over the North Western Motorway

3. Cross Oriel Avenue to path opposite and follow path straight ahead into St Margarets Reserve.

4. Go past Children's playground (on your left) and cross Fitzherbet Avenue and follow path straight ahead.

5. Cross Flaunty Place and join path behind the Flaunty Reserve playground going to the left < that goes up the hill.

6. At the end of the zig zag path turn right > into Elizabeth Drive and continue to Moire Road.

7. Cross Moire Road and follow path straight ahead.

8. Cross Brougham Place and follow path straight ahead.

9. Cross Rena Place and follow path straight ahead.

10. Turn left < West Harbour Drive.

11. Turn right > at the path just before Garcia Place (on left).

12. Cross the blue bridge, and follow the signpost to Manutewhau Walkway 30 minutes.

13. At the end of the next bridge continue straight ahead up the main track.

14. At the crossroads go straight ahead and follow signpost "to Manutewhau 20mins".

15. Turn right > along Moire Road.

16. Cross Moire Road at the Preschool and enter Manutewhau Reserve.

17. Continue along concrete path, (ignore path to left to bridge that goes to a playground and picnic site) at T-junction turn left <.

18. Cross over Holmes Drive to path opposite which comes out at the yellow bridge.

NB. If you wish start the walk from Moire Park entrance in Granville Drive, follow the track across the side of the sports field and join the Manutewhau Walk to the left. Follow directions from #15.

RESOURCES

Auckland Council – current dog regulations:

aucklandcouncil.govt.nz/EN/licencesregulations/dogsandanimals/
Pages/home.aspx

Dog friendly web sites:

doogle.co.nz
fetchmag.co.nz
planmyplay.co.nz/spotlight/auckland-special-interest-dog-
friendly-exercise-areas-beaches
localist.co.nz/auckland/articles/top-10-auckland-dog-parks

Dog friendly beaches and other areas. Please check Auckland Council website and signage for current regulations.

1. Takapuna, Cheltenham and North Head on the North Shore.
2. Kakamatua on Manukau Harbour.
3. Kauri Point on the North Shore.
4. Mission Bay and Kohimarama along Tamaki Drive.
5. Mellons Bay near Howick.
6. Taipari Strand, Taikata Road, Te Atatu Peninsula.

ABOUT THE AUTHORS

For many years, Helen and her friend Grace talked as they walked around Cornwall Park and One Tree Hill. One day, Grace turned to Helen and said "Would you like a change from walking around here?" Helen replied "Yes, but where would we go?"

And that was the beginning of the Mini Adventures for Maximum Enjoyment – for Health, Fitness and Fun. Grace scouted out the routes, the girls would get lost at times, but they walked on. And then Grace bought herself a smart phone and even though they still got lost, they could tell where they were from the map on the phone.

The walks had to comply with strict criteria – first of all, they had to be circular, each walk had to provide interest and a 'wow' factor, if there was a café nearby even better. But most of all, they had to be fun and enjoyable – not tedious.

The walks in this book have all been traversed (more than once) by Helen and Grace (and documented by Helen) so that the walker has very little chance of getting lost.

"Short Walks in Auckland website has been brilliant find for Sport Waitakere as we are both working towards a common goal."

**Emma Haigh | Active Communities Advisor |
Sport Waitakere**

On behalf of The University of Auckland, I would like to thank Helen for the custom route maps she has produced for our popular 'Walk the Talk' programme. The maps are perfect for our needs, professionally made and well received by participants.

**Hugh Markham, Active Recreation Manager,
The University of Auckland**

More walk guides available at
www.walksinauckland.co.nz

WHAT WALKERS ARE SAYING...

The thing I enjoy most about walking in Auckland is the variety. There are so many choices and you can have completely different surroundings on each walk.

The things we like most of walking in Auckland. - Auckland's diverse landscapes (beaches, bush, volcanoes and urban) offer superb variations to suit all ages, weather and abilities. We have beautiful spots to see, never too far from a coffee or lunch and get the added benefit of healthy exercise.

 All the lovely diverse views, hills, trees and parks, native bush, beach and sea side places

I enjoy the diversity of walks in Auckland, from bush walks to waterfront walks, heritage walks to walks through suburban streets, parks and cafes! There are always lots of new things to discover and explore.

This year we moved from the Netherlands to Auckland. Walking is a very good and pleasant way to explore our new home country. Short Walks in Auckland is a good help.

Walking with family, variation i.e. coastal, forest, volcanoes.

Being able to take in the vast variety of sights sounds and smells, Flora and Fauna, and its varying landscape.

62

I enjoy going for walks on Auckland's volcanoes, I have on occasions done a different volcano every day for a week or two with people who are recovering from mental illness and they found this very beneficial. Thank you for your very informative e-mails and walking guides.

The best thing about walking in Auckland is the variety, city walks, volcano walks, park walks, harbour walks, etc and you can never know what the weather will throw at you

As a fairly newly retired person, it is a great source of pleasure to me to have the time to walk.   Living in west Auckland there are many options and varieties to choose from.   However, I particularly enjoy the walks around Te Atatu Peninsula that give views of the city, quiet bird sanctuaries through coastal estuaries and there is always somebody to say hello to.

CURRENT TITLES IN THIS SERIES

Volcanoes
Coastal Walks (part one)
Coastal Walks (part two)
Urban Bush
Dog Friendly Walks (part one)
Dog Friendly Walks (part two)
Dog Friendly Walks (part three)
Best of the West
Best of the East
Best of the South
Best of the North

Available from Amazon.com and Auckland Libraries